DRY TEARS

KEVIN L. ALEEM

WITH COVER AND CHAPTER
ILLUSTRATIONS BY

SHAWN EVANS

Order this book online at www.trafford.com
or email orders@trafford.com

Most Trafford titles are also available at major online book retailers.

Print information available on the last page.

ISBN: 978-1-4251-0818-2 (sc)
ISBN: 978-1-4251-9314-0 (e)

Trafford rev. 10/18/2019

www.trafford.com
North America & international
toll-free: 1 888 232 4444 (USA & Canada)
fax: 812 355 4082

DEDICATION

MY ROOTS HAVE PROVIDED

THE LIFE AND OPPORTUNITY

TO CREATE THIS WORK

HOWEVER,

IT IS THE SEEDS OF

"TAKYMA,"

DAUGHTERS

TAKIA JANAE' ALEEM,

KYRA SHANI ALEEM,

& NEPHEW

MARQUIS ANTAE' HUDSON

THAT THIS WORK IS DEDICATED

&

WHO WILL CARRY ON THE LEGACY

LETTER FROM THE AUTHOR

First, let me express my thanks for your support of my passion. For the creation of poetry is a passion I have long held and at many times in my life masked with facades. Facades used to approach various issues, circumstances, and societal situations; I experienced growing up as an athlete, scholar, thug, and "wanna be," ladies man in Philadelphia.

As the cover of this work represents the concept of, "Dry Tears," was created to represent the emotions felt by males, but evaporated, dried, masked and flamed by the passions we feel and use as survival and tactical tools for navigating today's society.

Dry Tears approaches feelings and rhythms as they relate to how African American men may view or may be viewed by society, children, and issues thought but never spoken. I thought this would be thought provoking and conversation invoking to the reader.

I played peek-a-boo behind the façade in the, *"Life and Love"* section of my first book of poetry Through A Blackman's Eyes. However, I decided to do a full Phantom of the Opera mask rip in the, *"View of Hard and Soft Hearted Tears"* sections of Dry Tears, and expose what we really feel sometimes when it comes to the power the opposite sex has over our emotions. I even decided to create the parity to the poem, "Divorce" found in Through A Blackman's Eyes, and title it, "Marriage." These sections are truly designed to reach your heart as you experience this book.

I pray that my passion is enjoyed as you read this work, because my passion is meant to speak to all men and women of all hues. Reinstalling communication, speaking truth, removing misperception, and revealing love. Yes! We are capable of true love, compassion and excellence behind the many facades we present.

Dry Tears is meant to lay the gauntlet, set the bar, make the challenge, and speak the truths. We feel, we love, we hurt, we make many many many mistakes, we are proud, we are strong, we want it easy, we will take it hard, we are spiritual, we need guidance, we need love, we are men!

Thank You
Kevin L. Aleem

View of Contents

Chapter 1 – *THE VIEW OF SOCIETY*
PAGE-

1) Responsibility
2) Truth
4) Life's Disconnect
6) Accountability
7) The Nightmare Can Be A Dream

Chapter 2 - *THE VIEW OF THE CHILDREN / YOUTH*

8) Open Letter To An Absent Daddy
9) Life's Education
10) To The Top
11) Young Lesson
12) Adolescent Strife

Chapter 3 - *THE VIEW OF SOFT HEARTED TEARS*

13) The First Thing I Noticed
14) You Make Me Reach
15) What If
17) Please
18) The Toy
19) Funny Love
20) Black Man's Heart
21) Marriage
23) Widows Call
24) Why

Chapter 4 - *THE VIEW OF HARD HEARTED TEARS*

25) The Roses
27) When I Think Of You
28) Be Still, Be Quiet, & Think
29) Loves End

Chapter 5 - *THE VIEW OF MASKED UNSPOKEN THOUGHTS*

30) Alone
31) Patients Anxiety
32) Hypocrites Cry
33) The Desired Dog
35) Promise Of Tomorrow
36) Suicide
37) Thinking Life
38) Dry Tears

CHAPTER
1

THE VIEW OF SOCIETY

PAGE-
1) Responsibility
2) Truth
4) Life's Disconnect
6) Accountability
7) The Nightmare Can Be A Dream

RESPONSIBILITY

Blackman take back your family
Lead them as per God's grace
Don't buy the hype, or live the myth
Don't be a ghost, a thought, a space

Blackman lead your family
Always do better than you can
For society set the laws
Yet, the law of God made you a man

For here is a question on the leader
That God formed you to be
Are you weak enough to slap your woman?
Or strong enough to guide your child across your knee

Question yourself
Then ask yourself
Why?
Did God give you the strength from within?
These are the tools that make you go further
A father, a partner, a friend.

Fear to lead and fear to learn
For a Blackman with God is a folly
For fear mixed with the strength of God
Succeeds to make only the Devil Jolly

You weaken the link set up to provide
Guidance for the challenge you face
You are the head of your household
The mantle, the leader, the pace

Blackman take back your family
These words should never be said to you
For your family should never be left without the leader
God said it!
You know it!!
It's true!!!!

TRUTH

Society and it's changing attitudes and altitudes
Styles that seem foreign to see
Brothers with mixed up priorities and
Sistas that say, *"That's the man for me!"*

So fly young brother
Tell me what it is all about
Was that your new Benz I saw?
Parked at the local Laundromat

Blaming everything on the white man
Shouting it's his fault for all that is wrong
Yet, when it comes to your child's education
You think it's cute he knows all the words to the
"NIGGA This, NIGGA That" song

Call yourself a man
Clearly a father to your child
But he doesn't even know your name
And DAMN, DAMN, DAMN, He's wild

Society plays you as stars
Sipping champagne on the open seas
And will let you disrespect your Queens
As being pimped out on their knees

Still want to blame others for your troubles
When do you take a hard look at the me?
The skipping school, The hanging out, The easy money
WAKE UP, WAKE UP, WAKE UP, and **SEE**

To my beautiful baby black Queens
With everything hanging all out
You think the brothers are smiling because you look cute
But really, they're going
OOO,
AHH,
And Damn! I Wanna Shout

For I see all she has to offer
And there is no mystery to me
She don't deserve my respect
Because everyone sees
What should only be for me

For this life is not all give me
Own it,
Don't care
It is also
Responsibility, Challenge, Courage,
Trial, Peril, and mostly
Prayer

Society may be a changing
But we have the strength to change it back
Teach one
NO!
To a Lie
And
YES!
To a Truth
Restore the pride in being black

LIFE'S DISCONNECT

Looking straight up
While bowing straight down
Kneeling to the pressure
While standing my ground
Loving you - Yes!
While hating you - No!
Life's disconnect.
Which way do I go?

Angry all the time
With a smile on my face
Full from the passion
With no love in my space
Starving for nourishment
With the completion of a meal
Life's disconnect.
What's the damn deal?

Want to hold you tight
Just to push you away
Punished for my wrongs
Just no guilt today
Sing of praise by day
Just to sin at night
Life's disconnect.
What the hell is right?

Loving my woman
Through the jealousy and pain
Selling my pride
Through the ignorance and shame
Doing acts of clear wrong
Through words that seem right
Life's disconnect.
Why continue to fight?

Look into my eyes
Yet be blind to see
Know all about the person
Yet never know me
Raise a child the best you can
Yet fail them in the end
Life's disconnect.
Was it worth it all my friend?

Opposites repel,
Opposites attract
Opposites make life real
When you look to the
Life's disconnect.
You look to the reason to feel!

ACCOUNTABILITY

During our lust for life
We must be careful as we go our way
Remember the respect for others feelings
As we begin to play

Life is so beautiful
Though short it may be
Keep the thought of the ant crushed and
The butterfly set free

Each of us has a life pattern
Which we follow or it follows us
Look to the person on each side of you
One of whom you must trust

As we guide ourselves through life
So carefree, wild, and bold
Do we really remember the tragedies?
Or the things as a youth we are told

As we weep, enjoy, and pray
Do we remember that no man can grow alone?
Will we remember all the lives we've affected or hurt?
When its time to account for what we've reaped and sown

THE NIGHTMARE CAN BE A DREAM

Though I live in the nightmare
I still hold onto the dream

Why will you not greet me?
If I am different, we can find our commonality
If I scare you, we can resolve the fear
If I am handicapped, we can learn to accept it
Because though I live in the nightmare
I still hold onto the dream

Why will you not hold my hand?
If it is dirty, we can wash it
If it is diseased, we can cure it
If it is deformed, we can learn to accept it
Because though I live in the nightmare
I still hold onto the dream

Why will you not hug me?
If I smell, we can bathe
If I look angry, we can resolve the problem
If I am unattractive, we can learn to accept it
Because though I live in the nightmare
I still hold onto the dream

What about me makes me different from you?
For I have a color, as do you
For my skin feels, as does yours
For my heartbeats, as does yours

So though I live in the nightmare
You do as well

So as I hold onto the dream for me
I hold it for you as well
Therefore we both can learn to accept it
Thus turning this nightmare into our dream
A dream of acceptance, hope, and love,
For all our equality

CHAPTER 2

THE VIEW OF THE CHILDREN/YOUTH

PAGE-
8) Open Letter To An Absent Daddy
9) Life's Education
10) To The Top
11) Young Lesson
12) Adolescent Strife

OPEN LETTER TO AN ABSENT DADDY

Dear Daddy, life donor
One hell of a guy
Please explain to me this.
Why weren't you there?
Why was Mommy forced to lie?

I understand she was lots of trouble.
Caused you lots and lots of pain
But that mess was between you and her
All I wanted is for you to call out my name

For I see other children out with their fathers
And I know Mom just can't compete
So undo influence seeps in
I'm influenced by Mr. So in So, Him, What's Up, and Joe Bleep

Though in my heart I'm not willing
And to stay away from temptation I try
Dear Daddy your eyes I may have
But these are my tears that I cry

Dear Daddy you left me alone
For reasons long since rejected
Will I continue to grow?
Become, be allowed, be all that's expected

Dear Daddy you don't seem to understand

It's not the money for the rent
It's the time you should have spent
It's the knowledge of a life on the earth
It's the value of my heritage and worth
It's the other half of my life that makes me whole
It's the start of positive ego swole
It's the man that made me live
It's your turn to have something to give
This is what your time means to me

Damn Daddy it's time to wake up and see!

Dear Daddy be that one hell of a guy
Don't make Mommy continue to lie!!!!!!!!

8

LIFE'S EDUCATION

The education of the youth
Begins with the wisdom of the old
Take the time to listen
You don't know it all
You're that bold

Look around and open your eyes
At what wondrous sights you'll see
Older men guiding the path of the young
Preparing away for thee

The value of their words
Their life experiences
An education no class could ever give
The immeasurable value of this time
Is for the life you have yet to live

Valued older gentleman
Placid and settled in their ways
Taking on the fiery youth
The know it alls
Living in a got to have it now haze

These are the lessons of life
Much too valuable to spurn
Time to sit your young ass down
Time to listen and to learn

You cannot help but to learn a lesson
From the time older men spend here
They educate you on life
They teach you to listen and
Not just to hear

So remember to say "Thank You" to the wise old gentlemen
Take their word and apply them as you live
This should have taught you
You're too young to have it all
Yet, you're never too old to give

TO THE TOP

As you aspire to reach your goals
Just remember that there are tolls

And

As you fight to reach the top
Just remember the little steps you hopped

And

As you toil with the pain within
Just remember you can't always grin

And

As you lay face to the ground
Just remember don't stay down

And

As you falter and life slowly crumbles
Just remember that this is a part of life's stumbles

And

As you reach the point of good
Just remember how proud you stood

And

As you become the best you can be
Just remember to always be me

And

As you struggle and as you strife
Just remember that this is life

YOUNG LESSON

Come here, come here closely
Listen as I give you a word
There is nothing in this life
That momma gave me
That my black ass did not deserve

That included the pudding on Sunday night
Or the spanking before I went to sleep
I even remember the time I was so dirty
She took Brillo to the bottom of my feet

So to the little hoodlums, badasses, banshees,
And hoochie mammas of today
You need to follow the following advice and
Find yourself a church and pray

For if you know like I do
Momma of yesterday has become Big Mamma today
So remember what I said about church
Your only hope is stay on your knees and pray

For you see she is tired, beat up and down,
And damn sure has no time to play
So the spanking I got yesterday
May be a homicide if given today

So take the advice that I am giving
Clean out the wax and listen up today
Stop taking the world for granted
Young Future you've earned nothing
But the right to Learn How,
Do right,
Grow strong &
Pray!

ADOLESCENT STRIFE

As you look through eyes
Just beginning to see
The development of the internal
And external self called me

Your parents are there
So do as you are told
You're much too young
Too young to be bold

You will go through a time
When all is expected
Yet all that you try
Will be soundly rejected

So keep your head up
And take it in stride
This is apart of life
In which none of us hide

Though you feel the adult life
Is the dream that you seek
Your parents will still guide you
You're feeling so weak

For this is the process
Of growing you see
You're too old to be young
Yet, too young to be free

CHAPTER
3

THE VIEW OF SOFT HEARTED TEARS

PAGE-
13) The First Thing I Noticed
14) You Make Me Reach
15) What If
17) Please
18) The Toy
19) Funny Love
20) Black Man's Heart
21) Marriage
23) Widows Call
24) Why

THE FIRST THING I NOTICED

The glow in the eyes
The sparkle of the smile
The style of the hair
The shape of the figure
The force of the presence

FORETELL

The beauty of the mind
The strength of the soul
The intricacies of the intellect
The sensitivities of the emotions

These tangential insights
these spiritual auras

ARE THE GRASPING POINTS OF

My attention
My focus
My drive

SO THAT I MAY APPRECIATE

What I see
What I sense
What I perceive
To be that which I observed

Then begins the development of
The aesthetic art form that is you
And it is that work of art
That becomes

THE FIRST THING I NOTICED

YOU MAKE ME REACH

You make me reach
For the moon, the stars, and the sun
The mystery, the glory, and the heat
For you are my goals and aspirations

You make me reach
For and out to others
As my lover, my friend, or my stranger
For you could be my strength or my downfall

You make me reach
For my heart and my soul
The love and the conscience
For you are my feelings

You make me reach
For I feel heartache
And only intense love can cause heartache
For you are my love

You make me reach
Reach so far for you
That even when your not there
I still reach

WHAT IF

I talked with my woman
Used both my eyes and ears
Really Listened to my woman
To the words,
For the words,
Yes, the words,
I needed to hear

So, I listened to my woman
And she said
What if-

I make a mistake, hurt you real bad, make you just want to leave.
So I stayed real silent
Gave her a blanket, and held her till her fears were relieved

So, I listened to my woman
And she said
What if-

You find my hidden secrets, what I did bad, all of my sins of the past.
So I stayed real silent
Reached for her hand, and held it steady and fast.

So, I listened to my woman
And she said
What if-

I'm just a thrill, some time to kill, and not the true choice for you.
So I stayed real silent
Drew her a bath, and massaged her body with aloe and dew

So, I listened to my woman
And she said
What if-

15

I don't quite measure up to all you seem to adore
So I stayed real silent
Offered my hand, and danced her across the floor.

So, I listened to my woman
And she said
What if-

I'm not what you expect me to be
So I stayed real silent
Looked her dead in the eye, then held her real close to me

So, I said to my woman
Listen
What if-

God did not allow you to love me so much
She stayed real silent
Kissed me tender, and allowed our hearts to touch.

PLEASE

Please talk to me
Though I sometimes cause a strain
Please talk to me
Though I sometimes cause you pain

Please hold me
Even when I don't do right
Please hold me
Even when I struggle fuss and fight

Please listen to me
Though my words may babble on
Please listen to me
Though my thoughts may be very wrong

Please kiss me
Even when I deserve a slap
Please kiss me
Even when my ego is fat

Please tolerate me
Though I sometimes make you sick
Please tolerate me
Though I may not be your best pick

Please love me
For all I turn out to be
Please love me
For just being me!

Please!

THE TOY

I feel a tear
I'm trying so hard to hold it back, to deceive
It's putting pressure on my chest
The tear runs, I grieve

For I look out, on, upon it
And find it so hard to believe
My favorite toy has been broken
The tear runs, I grieve

Grown man crying
Something no other pain could not achieve
But the toy, the joy, the smile of my heart
Is broken
The tear runs, I grieve

Damn it! I did it! I did it!
Which makes it even harder to believe
I had my toy safely in my hand
Now it's broken
The tear runs, I grieve

My favorite plaything
The toy that makes me never want to leave
I took it for granted
Allowed it to be broken
The tear runs, I grieve

Sweetheart My Dear,
I hope that you hear
I'd rather repair than to grieve
For you are my toy
And to fix us with joy
I have to work hard, be careful and
Believe!

FUNNY LOVE

I once heard a man
Say a line I'll never understand
He told his lady, "I love you so!"
From dandruff to toe jam

I felt so vile and truly disgusted
That I thought he had a bad stroke
That in his brain a vessel had broken
And really impaired this bloke

He came to me, it was time to explain
That he felt such a blinding passion
That his love could light up a city street
Just like a Christmas of old fashion

He only wanted the world
To really and truly know
That through the good and the bad
He loved his lady so

So anytime in life
Should you hear true love spouted so free
Just take the beauty that is meant
And you may one day see

That if a man can say such things
That sounds so goofy and bad
You can take it for yourself
That this is the best love
He's ever had

BLACKMAN'S HEART

Think you're strong, cool,
and truly a cut above
Well you have not tasted the real world
until you have lost a true love!

Your Woman, Your Wife, Your Mother,
a beautiful lady only you can see.
That one true weakness
From which you will never be totally free

You play the role of invincible,
worry free, devil may care
Though without that special woman in your life
You're a shell, hollow, not there!

Master had his whip
Slavery bound us up in chains
Yet the loss of the women we love
Holds by far the greater pains

So here's the real deal Blackman!
The loss of a true love hurts from the start
We put on a mask, keep a straight face
But our women are the Achilles heel of our
Heart!

MARRIAGE

As I sit here with the kids
No time to be alone
With all the playing and the noise
I can't hear the music of the quiet storm

The kids have gotten to stereo
Now the rap music is on
No more time for quiet reflection
Listening to a mellow song

I stare out at the photographer
Who is standing straight ahead
Pictures for my desk
To keep my family in my head

I listen to the puppies' torture
As he whimpers away in fear
Just wishing, needing, and wanting
For my son to release his ear

Where did this pain come from?
And oh so oh why
Guess it's as simple as this.
All four kids on one poor thigh

My heart is beating fast
I hope it keeps going on
Because chasing after kids
The heart has got to be strong

I pray I never falter with
My greatest choice in life
I love all four kids
And my beautiful choice for wife

There is a tear that swells inside
That I want the world to see
I'm not crying for myself
But the pride of my family

It doesn't hurt at all
And it always feels so new
Yes, that deep down blinding passion
I feel for the children and you

Though sometimes my thoughts may wonder
They are always filled with you
Yes, I clearly realize that together my Dear
There is nothing we cannot do

WIDOWS CALL

Close your eyes
Remember the night, the dawn, the dusk, the day
The time and times we knew it was right
The times together we prayed

This is a call to my lady
Tell her heart all is all right
For an angel touched me
Told me to follow
Walk in Gods path to the light

My love for you and Gods love for you
Could never ever compare
But you need to know in your heart
Both will always be there

Look inside, look outside, Look all around
And you **Will Still** see me
Because though I now travel with the Father
My love resides within thee

So I send you a special message
From a level where we will once again meet
Close your eyes
Re-live our love
Until at the Fathers house
We once again speak

WHY

If my heart was a steaming pot
Could you handle the intensity of the pour?
Is your cup of Love deep enough,
Strong enough,
Heat resistant and more

I ask the question of which I have the answer
Not for test, trial, nor fear.
Yet, sometimes my Love
What my heart does know
My brain and ears must hear

For logic and reason, do not work with us
For trust and passion is our core
Though blind by passion
We see through trust
Thus, our lives as one should soar

Then why do we have issues?
Problems and negative expectations
When did our beautiful Love
Our special Kiss
Become tortured speculation?

Why place the challenges?
Play the games?
Tempt the love with War?
For our love is based on pleasure,
Comfort, need, and amore'

What's going on my Dear?
As I reflect upon
The intensity of my pour
Love me true
Love me direct
Ask me **"Why"** no more

CHAPTER
4

THE VIEW OF HARD HEARTED
TEARS

PAGE-
- 25) The Roses
- 27) When I Think Of You
- 28) Be Still, Be Quiet, & Think
- 29) Loves End

THE ROSES

I brought my lady some roses
Blood red, spectacular and bright.
My lady accepted these flowers
Yet, my meaning was lost in sight

Did I mean to bless our relationship?
Or were these the flowers of a funeral or more
To hide the mourning pain
Of the fact that I'm almost out the door!

Is my face still a mask?
Or through my eyes can she see
That I am a man tormented, conflicted
And as pained as a man in love can be!

My lady, my love, feelings are welling up so strong
Look at you lovingly, yet, insides so tight
Is it right for me to still love you?
When my heart has taken flight!

Am I soul searching?
Yes!
That's what it is for this man
I must be soul searching and that must be why
My love is making a last stand!

This is harder than any rock
Feels colder than the slice of a razors steel
Decisions about the future with my baby
Have to be a dream, it's so unreal

For you were all I ever wanted
My friend, my love or die
For you I was to be to the end of the fairy tale
The knight, the prince, the guy

Yet, I still am standing here
And it's time to finally speak
Yet, the words are caught in my throat
And the pain is making me weak

For the roses mean
Both funeral and love
For you and me, my friend
For I have been blessed
With our beautiful time together
Yet, I must bury our relationship
It's over, all done
THE END

WHEN I THINK OF YOU

When I think of you
Waves of emotions
My thoughts go through

Starting like an ocean
Cresting at high tide
Then like the receding water
There goes my heart and pride

When I think of you
My blood flows
As if in a butter churn
Its starts out thin and smoothly going
Then hardens clots, and soon ceases flowing

When I think of you
My face begins it's strange contorting
It goes from beautiful smile
To cold frown
From gentle breathing
To harsh snorting

When I think of you
My mind realizes the reality and truth
Of the thin line
Between terrible and great
Between joy and pain
Between love and hate

When I think of you
I realize
That you are
What I want
Yet someone I should never have

So for your sake
So for my sake
I'll just think of you

BE STILL, BE QUIET, THINK

Another argument with my lady
Tension, yet this is no surprise
Repeat problems, and issues
Solved, yet still to be reprised

Be Still, Be Quiet, & Think because the truth never lies

Cannot be forgiven of sin
If sin can never be forgot
Perception of guilt in your eyes
Reality of innocence is not

Be Still, Be Quiet, & Think before the pain becomes a clot

Hanging on through the hang ups
Calling back just to hear the click
How long do I truly stay?
When you say I am making you sick

Be Still, Be Quiet, & Think before things get worse quick

The question of why are we together
When constant struggle is our fate
Am I strong enough to say good-bye?
Or too weak to say it's too late

Be Still, Be Quiet, & Think before our love turns to hate

I love you with all of my heart
Give you every thing that I can
Yet, just a simple conversation with you
Leaves me feeling less than man

Be Still, Be Quiet, & Think please listen and understand

We need to stop the drama
We have gone far past the brink
Be Still My Love
Be Quiet My Heart
Take The Time and Think!

LOVES END

Lying in my bed
Dreaming though not quite asleep
Feeling so many things yet, feeling nothing
But my façade has begun to weep

Looking over to my woman
Loving thought
Shallow yet So So deep
Wondering about the promises
Once made
The promises I reluctantly keep

For unhappiness has griped me
It has bound me in so many ways
That if cupid was to shoot a new arrow
Of love
Could it penetrate this concrete maze?

Reasons to stay
Reasons to go
Reasons none the less
Reasons turn to excuses
For this is a terrible mess

See life, love, and breakup
Are fueled by negativity
Pile it on, build it up and
Boom!
The end of a special we

You may one day truly claim
You never saw it coming
But the true reality is
Its presence was always there
Like a fly in your eardrum humming

So as I lay here looking at you
Loving you still
Preparing to say that it's over my friend
Dear Lord give her the words
That will make me think thrice
Or allow it to just be Love's End

CHAPTER
5

THE VIEW OF MASKED UNSPOKEN THOUGHTS

PAGE-
- 30) Alone
- 31) Patients Anxiety
- 32) Hypocrites Cry
- 33) The Desired Dog
- 35) Promise Of Tomorrow
- 36) Suicide
- 37) Thinking Life
- 38) Dry Tears

ALONE

Here I am
Alone once again
The bluest of blue
In deep need of a friend

Though I may be alone
And damn it's a terrible fright
Can't place the blame on others
Time to look at myself
Build from within and right

In my time alone
Will I be to blind to see
To use this time
To help build me

No need to be lonely
Just living in my blue
Time to make myself better
For a stronger me, with or without you

Though I may be alone
Blue and needing a friend
I still have a life to live
Though alone
I shall
BEGIN

PATIENTS ANXIETY

As I lay here in the hospital
And it is extremely plain to see
That the nurses and doctors are caregivers
That they are here to help me

My problem is, I never learned to trust much in life
Whether it be friend, family, or foe
Then I end up injured and ill
I now must trust those I don't even know

This is a process of education
This is a new time to learn
This is the assistance of strangers
This is help my injured and ill ass cannot spurn

I have many fears about the condition
That brought me to this place
Will I live to see the outside?
The beautiful wide-open space

Early morning awakening
Thermometer poked in and out
Check your wound? Change your dressing?
Dear Lord I want to shout

I learned to lust my nurse
My angel of mercy so dear
I hope she realizes that this is temporary
Just a manifestation of my fears

This is a scary time in my life
Placed in a bed down and out
I fear for my condition
Who do I trust? And
When do I get out?

These are a few of the feelings
That has a strong grip on me
Please doctors say I'm ok
Sign my discharge
Let me go free...

HYPOCRITES CRY

Peace be with you
And all praises unto the Lord
These are the phrases
Through my youth, I am forged

Yet, as I look all around me
Just up and down my street
I see the blood of precious life
As violence turns human flesh into simply meat

How can peace be with me
Tis true it's a strange thought
When all I've gotten in life
Was gained though struggle and as I fought

I thank the Lord
And each and every day I pray
I ask for forgiveness
To take my sins away

Yet, I watch the Preacher standing in the pulpit
Preaching the word till it hurts
But I watch his eyes closely
As they look up each and every skirt

Well couldn't this be called
The greatest hypocrites cry?
I pray for forgiveness
Then look square into the lie

So I ask this special question
As I contemplate my fate
Can I follow the word
And make the praise?
Or for this Blackman is it just
Too Late!

THE DESIRED DOG

I kissed my women gently and
Two seconds after we pulled away
I looked in her eyes and feared the thought
Wanted to run, to hide
To Pray

For I knew what was coming
For I see it every time that we meet
My baby is never satisfied in the present
It is the future that she wants us
To speak

What's next?
Where are we going?
Are you going to make an honest woman of me?
If not my brother!
Then this milk is no longer free!

I grab my head and say
What's up?!!!
Where did all this come from?
We where in the midst of a loving kiss
Now its drama on the run

Now look here Woman!
Listen well
For I won't be saying this twice
I like things just as they are
And if you don't then here is my advice

Step up, step off, or just turn around
For this game will no longer be played
The rules for our relationship
At the beginning
Had clearly been laid

I did not lie
I told you true
I was not about to commit
So please stop pressing me when you feel the guilt
Of, "you gotta make me legit"

The truth is girl
Respect was played
When you gave up on yourself my friend
Where was all this drama
When you let me hit it
And get in the wind

Check yourself Lady
And check yourself fast
Before things get out of hand
I know I'm a dog
I know I do wrong
But you want me for your man!

PROMISE OF TOMORROW

My God, My God!
Thank you, for the lesson of the day

The valued lesson of capturing memories
By living through your blessed ways

For I was an unfocused wonderer
Seeking what will always happen next

Never happy with the here and now
Never appreciating being blessed

Worry and wonder were my motto
Apprehension and expectation, my cheer

Always looking to the promise of tomorrow
Waiting for my needs to be filled and come to me here

Well now as I lay here touching your hand
With no more promises of tomorrow

I wish I had learned, enjoyed, and appreciated much earlier
I wish I had learned to follow

I would have enjoyed the days and praised the nights with the
Promise of Tomorrow

I would have made the memories with the
Promise of Tomorrow

Please forgive me my God and teach others about the
Promise of Tomorrow

Live Today
Remember Yesterday
For The
Promise of Tomorrow

SUICIDE

Suicide: The one time only act of a one second

Hero

Suicide: The master eraser of beautiful

Memories

Suicide: The cowards way to express

Courage

Suicide: The total disregard for the world's greatest potential

You

Suicide: The strongest and strangest way to say I can't

Win

Suicide: The creation of pain for us left to carry

On

Suicide: The quest for peace by quitting its only hope

Life

Suicide: The worst answer to all of life's

Questions

Suicide: The lie of

Love

Suicide: The removal of life's power from the guidance of

GOD

THINKING LIFE

As an organ may hum
As a choir may sing
As a child may cry
Unknown is what life may bring

These are a few of the thoughts
That through my mind may run awry
They bring the joy to my smile
They bring the tear to my eye

As I think is as I am
This statement is true, so true
Yet many a thing in this life
Shall my thoughts and being go through

The confusion of it all
Make life appear as a dream
Yet, just try to awaken yourself
To find all is as it seems

So to sit back and think through life
Means nothing more than to ponder
It doesn't resolve problems or needs
It just leaves your mind to wonder

So to think your way through life
Is to throw all of its challenges away
Live and love through the challenges
Make sure you live completely
Everyday!

DRY TEARS

Eyes wide open
Praying for no fears
Cleared my mind to the reality of a Black Man
Shed the first of my
Dry tears

Time to face the world
To be tried and tried again
Respect the pain propaganda of my enemy
Yet, ignore the murder of my friend

For my society is not ready to understand me
For there is more to this Black Man than can be seen
I have been told all about myself
Been researched, dissected, demeaned

Told that a school system educates me
Gave me a month dark, cold, and blue
But the history book forgot all about me
Forgot about everything that was true

Living with a brain disrespected
Speaking four languages just to survive
Need the kings English for my job at the restaurant
Then at home, in the hood, and at the club
I need Ebonics, Hip Hop, and Jive

You wonder why I stroll
Smooth up and down my street
Part is due to my rhythm
Part is due to the glass at my feet

My bowed head should not be taken as a sign of submission
It's more like studying or praying my friend
Or a Black Man requesting strength, restraint,
Or simply the Creators permission

I am all, I am nothing,
I am the world in just one
For I walk toward the Creator,
Hand in hand with the Son

Society has been trying for ages
To see a strong black man cry
Well they have yet to earn that privilege
Not with a whip, a torture, nor a lie

The world may never earn that privilege
Of seeing the moisture flow from my eyes
Just know that I enjoyed the beauty,
Endured the Pain,
And YES!
OH YES!
I was alive!

So when the time does come to say farewell
To all these earthly fears
Let them know that my eyes closed
And all I cried were just a few
DRY TEARS!

Printed in the United States
By Bookmasters